Bipolar Disorder Guide

Know myths and truths about it, and live confidently ever after

AMARPREET SINGH

THE THOUGHT FLAME
TURNING SPARK INTO FLAME

info@thethoughtflame.com

www.thethoughtflame.com

Table of Contents

Introduction

I know that when many of us get diagnosed with having something as serious as bipolar disorder, we often feel that the best thing for us to do is to give up. I am here to tell you that you life does not need to stop simply because of this disorder.

In order for you to live with this illness and to overcome the power and control that is currently has on your life, you need to accept this inescapable fact: you are much greater than this illness and you have the power to overcome it. No matter how difficult it may seem to wrap your head around all of the problems and challenges that you are experiencing in your life, you need to believe with every fiber of your body that you deserve to live the happy and productive life that you deserve.

Remember, if you do not develop the strength

to want to help yourself, you will forever be trapped within this debilitating illness and never find the strength to move on with your life.

Now is the time for you to become the person that you want to be and find the strength to conquer this mental illness. From the moment that you accept that this suffering does not need to become a normal part of your life, the faster you can begin living the life that you want.

In this book you will learn to do exactly that and will find proven tips and strategies to survive bipolar and to live a healthy and productive life that you deserve. I hope that by the end of this book you learn that you can live the life that you want to live and finally take the steps towards living that life, in a much happier and healthier way.

So, what are you waiting for? Let's get started!

Chapter One: Know What Treatment Options Are Available To You

When you have been diagnosed with bipolar disorder, your doctor might have already informed you that you may need to take medications for the rest of your life. Medication which has been established as the primary treatment for bipolar disorder aims to help you control or even eliminate the signs and symptoms of your disorder so you can maintain a "symptom-free" state. The medications basically work to prevent you from getting a manic or depressive episode relapse.

However, there are still no definite guidelines that can help your doctor to accurately determine the right kind and right dosage of medications for you. Some people respond very well on a certain type of medication without experiencing any severe side effects. Other people, on the other hand, may respond better on other types. Because of this, you need to work close with your psychiatrist so he or she can assist you in trying out different combinations until you get the right one for you. You need to keenly observe the effects of the medications that you take so you can present them to your doctor who can analyze it for you.

Here are a few ways that you can effectively manage your medication and hopefully you will find these tips to be rather useful.

1. In case you notice that there are certain side effects that start to develop, you should immediately consult your doctor to seek guidance on the next steps that you need to do. But you are strongly warned not to abruptly stop taking your medications when you notice

the side effects without talking to your doctor first. When you abruptly stop your medications, you can trigger either a manic or depressive episode attack.

2. You will need to make sure that you advise your doctor of any other prescribed medications that you are taking to make sure that none of them can negatively interact with your bipolar disorder medications. There are certain medications that can actually slow down the treatment of your bipolar disorder and there are others which can even cause you to poorly respond to the medications which will then lead to a longer period of psychiatric hospitalization.

3. Always remember that the medications prescribed to treat your bipolar disorder are all powerful drugs. You cannot take for granted your doctor's exact instructions when taking your medications to make sure that you only

not get the most benefit from them, but more importantly, that your health will not be put in danger. You need to make the effort of carefully noting down the symptoms and any side effects that you might be feeling after taking the medications.

4. To ensure that you will be able to effectively manage your bipolar disorder medications, you will need to carefully monitor any of the symptoms and side effects that you might observe while taking the medications. This will enable your doctor to correctly adjust the kinds of medications you are taking, the dosages or both.

5. As much as possible, avoid intake of alcohol and illegal drugs while you are under medication for your bipolar disorder because they can make your bipolar disorder medications not only to become ineffective but may also trigger increased negative side effects.

Research studies show that people suffering from bipolar disorder who also have alcohol or drug addiction have higher risks of relapse and recurrence of both manic and depressive episodes.

Following these guidelines will help to ensure that you are dealing with your bipolar disorder in a way that will leave you having many better days than bad days. I highly advise that you follow all of these tips to the T if you want to see any changes in how you are feeling right away.

Chapter Two: Common Myths About Bipolar Disorder and The Truth Behind It

There are a variety of myths out there regarding this disorder that it is most likely to confuse people suffering with the illness than help them. Of course behind every myth there is a corresponding truth to it and in this chapter I am here to set the truth straight.

Myth #1: An Individual's Mood is the Only Thing that Gets Affected

Most people believe that the only thing that gets affected if a certain individual has bipolar disorder is the mood, but the truth is it affects the entire life of the sufferer . It affects one's memory, thinking, concentration, energy level, sleep patterns, judgment , sex drive, confidence, and even appetite. Moreover, the disorder has also been linked to substance abuse, diabetes, migraine, heart disease, anxiety and hypertension.

Myth #2: Medications are the only thing that can Keep Bipolar Disorder Symptoms Under Control

It is true that medications can help keep the symptoms at bay, but self-help strategies, therapy, support from loved ones, and having healthy habits (like following a well-balanced diet) also assist in keeping the symptoms of bipolar disorder under control. Doing worthwhile activities (such as working out and creating works of art) help the sufferer take his or her mind off the disorder. In other words, having fun is a good alternative to drugs.

It is also important to avoid stress. When the sufferer is feeling stressed, they can use simple strategies, such as getting a relaxing massage, listening to calming music, or immersing the body in a tub of warm water with some drops of aromatic oil. Aromatic scents can also help ease the mind and body.

Myth #3: The Sufferer will not be able to Recover or Live Normally

The truth is that there are people with bipolar disorder (some of them are famous celebrities) who have happy family lives, successful jobs, and almost-perfect relationships. These people experienced some difficulties at one point, but bipolar disorder did not stop them from living fulfilling lives.

Living with bipolar is not easy and, in fact, it can be very challenging, but it is not something that can stop anyone from having a normal life. Solid support from family and friends, together with the proper treatment, a healthy lifestyle, and good coping skills, can help the victim a lot. Anyone with the dreadful disorder can still live a normal and happy life while keeping the symptoms at bay.

Myth #4: A Person who has Bipolar Only Lives with Alternating Episodes of Depression and Mania

The truth is that although there are times when a bipolar disorder sufferer may only seem to have alternating episodes of mania and depression. However , it does not mean that the sufferer will be like this for the rest of their life. Such occurrences do not last for long, especially if the patient gets correct treatment and receives support from both family and friends. There are times when mania or depression does not occur at all.

Sometimes, mania can be so subtle that it goes unnoticed. There are also cases where people with bipolar disorder can go for days or weeks without showing symptoms.

All of the myths that you just learned about are

for the most part absolutely baseless. The only important thing that you need to know is that will the support of positive people in your life, the use of modern medicine and the willpower to overcome your illness, will you be able to live the life that you have always wanted to live.

Chapter Three: Types of Bipolar Disorder and Common Triggers

The truth of the matter is that bipolar disorder is an illness than is easily manageable. There are many different types of bipolar disorder and each type of bipolar disorder can be identified by the different episodes a person may go through. Knowing the difference between the different types of bipolar disorder and what commonly triggers each type can help you find ways to cope with the episodes in a much more effective way.

Bipolar Type I

This type of bipolar depression is often associated with both mania and depression. This type is considered to be the most classic form of bipolar disorder today and it is also considered to be one of the most severe types. So, what is it about this type that differentiates it from the other types? It induces at least a single manic or mixed episode. A large number (not all) of bipolar I sufferers have also experienced episodes of major depression.

Bipolar Type II

This type of bipolar involves hypomania and depression. A manic episode does not occur. Instead, bipolar II entails recurring episodes of hypomania (the gentler form of mania) and major depression . To be diagnosed with bipolar II disorder, the patient must have gone through at least one episode of major depression and one episode of hypomania. If a manic episode occurs, it only means that the patient has bipolar I disorder and not just bipolar II.

Cyclothymia

This type is often characterized by mild depression and hypomania. It is considered the mildest of all types of bipolar disorder. It involves cycles of mood swings. In spite of this, the alternating moods are not harsh enough to be considered major depression or mania. To be diagnosed with this type of bipolar disorder , the patient must have undergone several episodes of mild depression and hypomania within two years. To prevent cyclothymia from turning into a full-blown bipolar disorder, it should be closely monitored and treated accordingly.

What Is The Difference Between Bipolar and Depression?

Bipolar disorder is usually mistaken as depression because sufferers typically seek help when they are already in depressive stage.

During manic episodes, patients fail to recognize that there is already a problem. Moreover, a number of people with bipolar are often more depressed than hypomanic or manic.

Know that the treatment for bipolar disorder is different from those for regular depression. The patient can end up in a risky situation if misdiagnosed. The antidepressant medication that is suitable for treating depression is potentially harmful to patients who have bipolar disorder. It is of utmost importance to choose a doctor who is well versed in treating the said disorder and knows how to recognize symptoms quickly.

Special Indicators To Use To Distinguish Between Bipolar and Depression

At a glance, bipolar disorder and depression

can seem to be the same. It really is difficult to tell them apart. Luckily, there are indicators that can help solve the mystery and put an end to the dilemma. The following symptoms are the things to watch out for, as they're signs of bipolar disorder that aren't usually exhibited by those suffering from depression:

1. The person has gone through recurring episodes of major depression.

2. The initial episode of major depression happened before turning twenty-five years old.

3. When not in a depressive state, that person's energy and mood levels are usually higher than those of most individuals.

4. Someone in the family (or a first-degree relative) has had bipolar disorder.

5. The episodes of major depression usually last for less than three months (considered short).

6. The sufferer usually loses his or her grip on reality every time an episode of depression occurs.

7. If the patient had experienced postpartum depression, then he or she is more likely to develop bipolar disorder later

The treatments for bipolar disorder are also very different from those made for depression. In fact, the medications that are usually given to someone who is suffering from depression do not apply to patients with bipolar disorder. It is also foolish to self-medicate. Sufferers must consult a doctor as soon as possible to avoid developing further complications.

The Common Trigger of Bipolar Disorder

Triggers are events, feelings or situations that can set off an episode. The best way to avoid this happening is to educate yourself on ways to deal with triggers when they occur as well as being aware of what your own personal triggers are. Many people keep a diary or journal to help them with this, as it can be a very personal thing. What can trigger one person into an episode might not bother another person with the same disorder.

If you can pinpoint exactly what it is that sets you off then you can work on this (both on your own and with your psychiatrist, family and friends) and figure out ways to either avoid the situation or to deal with it better when it does occur.

Some of the most common triggers that are often associated with a depressive episode can include:

- Anxiety or feeling anxious
- Stress

- Fighting with a loved one
- Financial problems
- The end of a relationship
- Changes in medication; not taking it, needing an increase in it etc
- Drug or alcohol abuse
- Changes in weather (depression is more common in winter)
- Other events that can leave you feeling stressed, worried or hurt

Some of the most common triggers that are often associated with a manic or hypomanic episode can include:

- Stress
- Fighting with a loved one
- Financial problems
- The end of a relationship
- Lack of sleep
- Not eating properly

- Changes in medication; forgetting or not taking it, etc.
- Drug or alcohol abuse
- Changes in weather (mania is more common in spring)
- Other events that make you feel stressed, anxious, angry

Chapter Four: Learn How To Deal With The Things That Will Stress Your Mind Out

It has been found that the most stressful and demanding events that occur in our everyday lives can play a critical role in how the symptoms of this disorder affects you. It has also been found that the way you can avoid an episode or attack is possible to achieve if you only learn how to control your everyday stress levels.

People with bipolar disorder are normal people, just like anybody else and they go through the same problem as everybody else: worrying about their family, worrying about their health and stressing over their financial future. The best way to manage and control your stress levels is to use your God given skills to help deal with the problems that arise in your life on a daily basis.

In this chapter you will learn different methods that you can use to help manage your stress and to have fewer depressive and manic attacks every single day.

The Best Way To Cope With Your Stressors

Step One: Identify Your Stressors-You will only be able to identify and define your problems if you are aware of the fact that problems do exist and they will inevitably come into your life. There are a variety of both internal and external signals that can be useful in identifying a problem as it occurs.

Your internal signals can include changes in your physical body like tension in your muscles, constant headache, changes in how you breathe and tension in your chest. These changes in your physical body can work as signals of stress that can prompt you that you have unsolved problems that require your attention. You can also observe changes in your emotions such as feeling hopeless and being anxious and worried. These changes in your emotions can also prompt you that you have existing unsolved problems.

Step Two: Prioritize Your Issues-It is quite common for people suffering from bipolar disorder to go through major problems after a dramatic manic or depressive episode. For instance, you may be faced with financial issues when you become unemployed as a result of your constant fatigue and low enthusiasm during a depressive episode.

Similarly, a manic episode can make you go through expensive shopping sprees that can also result to financial issues that you will have to deal with after the manic episode has passed. You may feel frustrated, hopeless and overwhelmed when you realize the gravity of your problems and you might be tempted to think that it doesn't seem possible to solve your problems especially when you cannot think of the right place to start.

Step Three: Determine What Your Coping Resources Are-Your coping resources are basically internal and external assets that you can call upon to help you to conquer the priority problems that you have identify. Your external assets or resources include support from other people who understand your predicament such as your loved ones, your doctor and your colleagues from work.

You can also get support from people who are not directly connected to you such as support agencies and your own financial assets. Your internal assets or resources include your own intelligence, creativity, determination, ingenuity, sense of humor and compassion, among other.

Step Four: Determine What Problems Can Block Your Coping Resources- Whether you like it or not, you will also encounter stumbling blocks that will hinder you from effectively coping with your problems. These stumbling blocks can also be both internal (such as limiting beliefs, impaired judgment and fearfulness) and external (such as tight deadlines, inadequate resources, and lack of information). You need to determine your own stumbling blocks so you can minimize them as you try to solve your problems.

Step Five: Overcome The Obstacles That Block Your Coping Resources-After you have determined your own stumbling blocks, it is quite essential that you face them and think of ways on how you can conquer them so you can better cope with your problems. There may be times when you may have to challenge your own beliefs to get past your stumbling blocks. Always keep in mind that it is ok to seek assistance or advice from other people.

Chapter Five: Ways To Successfully Manage Your Illness

While living with bipolar disorder is something that can be extremely difficult to deal with, even for the best of us, does not mean that it is not manageable. In this chapter you will learn different ways that you can help yourself to manage your illness and give yourself the chance to live the life you have always to live.

1. Make Sure That You Get Enough Sleep

Ensure you sleep properly. If possible be in bed by no later than 10pm and wake around 6am or 7am. Keeping a regular sleep schedule is essential in maintaining your moods and also preventing mania. It will also help regulate your body clock, which also plays a large part in your moods.

2. Eat As Healthy As Possible

Eat a healthy diet including plenty of fresh fruits and vegetables. High GI foods, complex carbohydrates and high sugar foods can mess up your moods severely.

3. Make Sure That You Get Adequate Exercise

As well as releasing feel good chemicals in your brain, it'll help you regulate your moods and if you are feeling manic burn up some of that extra energy. The best way to get the exercise that you need is to try a few relaxation techniques. Learning relaxation techniques to help manage your stress levels and moods. When you are uptight, anxious and stressed your arousal levels are higher which can lead to lack of sleep and can be a trigger for an episode.

4. Accept The Things That You Cannot Change

Accept that there are some things you can't do and reduce your stress levels. Stress is a major trigger for an episode. Reducing your stress levels may include things like reducing the hours you work, not taking on more than you can handle etc.

5. Make A Routine For Yourself

Proper time management will allow you to do things such as reduce your stress levels, get enough sleep, exercise and all sorts of other things. Building a regular routine will also help your moods.

6. Take All Of Your Medication Properly

Take your medications properly, at the correct times and do not skip doses or suddenly stop taking them – even if you do start feeling better. If you struggle to remember to take them tips to help you remember include keeping a list of the medications you are on, getting a pill case, setting alarms in your phone and keeping them somewhere highly visible (but out of reach of little hands if you have children).

7. Avoid Using Drugs or Alcohol

While I know that you may believe a six-pack can cure pretty much anything, alcohol and drugs as they can trigger episodes. Also if you are medicated, they can interfere with your medication. I highly suggest avoiding alcohol and drugs including caffeine, nicotine, and even some cold and flu drugs. Check with your doctor or pharmacist before taking ANY over the counter medications.

8. Surround Yourself With Positive People

Surrounding yourself with people that are negative will do nothing for you except bring you down and can possibly make your condition much worse. Avoid alcohol and drugs including caffeine, nicotine, and even some cold and flu drugs. Check with your doctor or pharmacist before taking ANY over the counter medications.

Join a support group and talk to others who understand what you are going through.

9. Be Open About Your Illness and Educate Yourself As Much As Possible On It

Be open and honest with your doctor as well as your family and friends. Be sure to also take on board what they say in relation to your disorder or behavior, often those closest to you can recognize symptoms of an episode before you can.

I also recommend that you educate yourself about your disorder, how to identify triggers, different medications and therapy. Knowledge is a weapon. Exercise regularly and maintain a healthy diet.

Conclusion

I want to sincerely thank you for downloading this book. With this book I hope that you have learned more about bipolar disorder and learned how to better cope with the symptoms of this illness.

If you are suffering from bipolar disorder, do not lose hope. I know that it can be hard to deal with your episodes, but you deserve happiness just like the rest of the human population. With this book I hope you have learned how to cope with your symptoms and have gained the confidence that you need to conquer this illness.

So, what is next? Well, the next step for you is to use the information that you have gotten from this book and put it to good use. Begin implementing the different strategies outlined in this book and begin managing your illness so that you can begin living the life you are entitled to.

About Us

The Thought Flame is committed to add value to its customers through various books, online courses and other resources. You can learn more about us and our books at www.thethoughtflame.com.

Don't forget to check out our amazing **online video courses** at www.thethoughtflame.com/courses/ to take your knowledge to another level.

To check out our **extraordinary collection of diet/cookbooks**, visit http://www.thethoughtflame.com/category/non-fictional/cookbooks/ .

As a part of our valued relationship with our customers, we keep providing you free promotional books, courses and other stuff on subscribing with us on our site. We have a strict anti-spam policy and assure you no spam mails will be sent to your mailbox.

To subscribe with us, visit

www.thethoughtflame.com.

Like our work and would like to say thanks?

Buy us a cup of coffee at

www.thethoughtflame.com/coffee/

Author

Amarpreet Singh is an avid learner and his passion for education has made him travel, work and study all across the world. He holds three masters degrees, including MBA, from top universities in Asia.

He is author of dozens of books, many of which are Amazon's bestseller, varying in various topics and categories. He also teaches many online courses having thousands of students across the world.

He has a keen interest in international affairs, economics, global poverty and politics, financial markets and entrepreneurship, and strives to be part of a community that shares the same passion.

He has worked as consultant with organizations like Airbus and The World Bank.

He loves travelling and learning about new cultures, and has been fortunate to live/work/travel/study in countries like India, China, Korea, US, South Africa, Japan, Philippines, Singapore, Canada etc., and learn about the culture and lifestyle in each of them.

To check out more of his work, visit

www.thethoughtflame.com

www.ingramcontent.com/pod-product-compliance
Lightning Source LLC
Chambersburg PA
CBHW020906310526
45786CB00018B/1898